D0872352

WILD WEATHER

JOHN PERRITANO

red rhino books®

NONFICTION

3D Printing

Area 51

Bioweapons

Cannibal Animals

Cloning

Comet Catcher

Drones

Fault Lines

Gnarly Sports Injuries

Great Spies of the World

Hacked

Little Rock Nine

Medal of Honor

Monsters of the Deep

Monsters on Land

The Science of Movies

Seven Wonders of the
   Ancient World

Tuskegee Airmen

Virtual Reality

Wild Weather

Witchcraft

Wormholes

SADDLEBACK
EDUCATIONAL PUBLISHING
www.sdlback.com

ISBN-13: 978-1-68021-051-4
ISBN-10: 1-68021-051-3
eBook: 978-1-63078-370-9

Printed in Malaysia

22 21 20 19 18   1 2 3 4 5

TABLE OF CONTENTS

Chapter 1
A STORM RAGES

The sky is dark.
Clouds roll in.
A siren howls.
Danger is near.

The wind spins.
A cloud forms.
It makes a funnel.

Take cover!
The family runs.
They go to the basement.

The *tornado* hits.

It lifts a car.

Power lines bend.

Wires snap.

Sparks fly.

The storm roars.

It sounds like a train.

The house shakes.

Windows break.

Wood snaps.

Glass shatters.

Then it is quiet.

Everything stills.

The family climbs out.

They look around.
The house is gone.
They look up.
Clouds part.
The sun comes out.
It is over.

Chapter 2
HOW'S THE WEATHER?

The wind blows.
It gets hot.
Rain pours.
Snow piles up.
Weather is part of life.

It starts with the sun.
The sun shines.
It heats Earth.
Some places get more sun.
Others get less.
More sun means warm weather.
Less means cool weather.

The air has *currents*.
These move air around.
Hot air rises.
It sucks air from below.
Cold air sinks.
It pushes air out.

This makes weather.
One place is sunny.
Another is cloudy.
Some places get rain.
Others get snow.

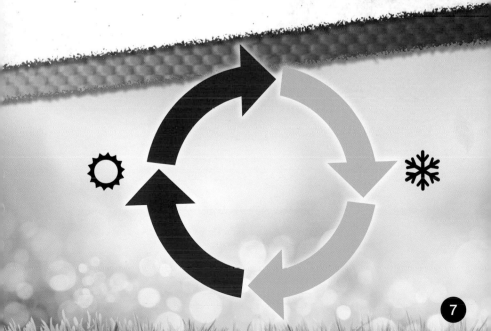

Weather makes a *climate*.
But the two are not the same.
Climate is an average.
It is weather over time.
Weather is what happens in the moment.

People study weather.
We call them *meteorologists*.
They use special tools.
These track weather.
Thermometers record temperature.

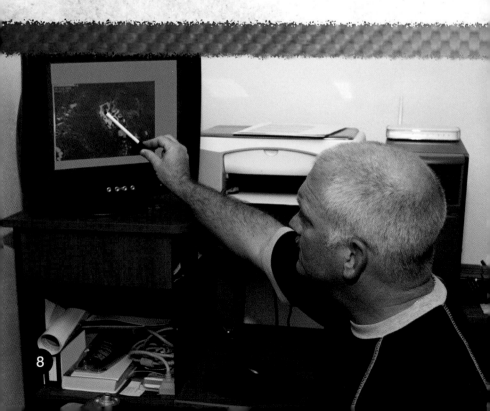

Wild Weather

The scales of a pinecone will close when it is going to rain.

Barometers measure pressure.

Satellites show images.

These tools help *forecast*.

People know what is coming.

They can get ready.

It can save lives.

9

Many places get rain.

It is not a big deal.

But it can turn deadly.

It was August 29, 2005.

There was a *hurricane*.

It was named Katrina.

The winds were strong.

They were 140 mph.

This is miles per hour.

The storm hit New Orleans.

Roofs were ripped off.

Cars flew.

Big trucks were tossed around.

The ocean was wild.
Huge waves came ashore.
Levees broke.
Water rushed into the city.

Hurricanes happen near the US.
They are in the Atlantic Ocean.
The Pacific has them too.
They are in other places.
But they have different names.
Some say *typhoons*.
Others say *cyclones*.

Hurricanes are bad storms.
They form in very warm water.
There is a season.
It goes from June to November.
That is when the water is warmest.

Hurricanes start simply.
Wind blows across the ocean.
Water *evaporates* from the wind.
It rises and cools.
Then it turns back into drops of water.
Storm clouds are formed.

Super Typhoon Yolanda hit the Philippines on November 14, 2013.

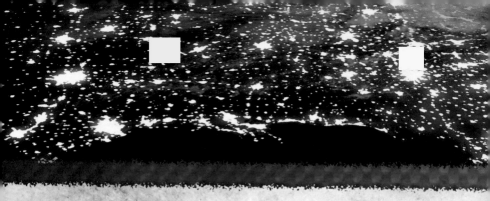

Storm clouds grow.

They rotate.

The cycle goes on.

The system moves in a circle.

Now it is a tropical depression.

It can grow into a tropical storm.

The center is still and calm.

This is called the eye.

Thunderstorms surround it.

Wind blows faster than 74 mph.

Then it is a hurricane.

The Florida coastline was pounded by Hurricane #9 of the 1945 season

Wild Weather

2017 saw a deadly hurricane season. It included Hurricane Harvey hitting the Texas coast in late August. More than 50 inches of rain flooded Houston. Hurricane Irma hit Florida a few days later. It caused one of the largest mass evacuations in history.

Hurricane Categories

Category	Wind Speed
1	From 74 to 95 mph
2	From 96 to 110 mph
3	From 111 to 130 mph
4	From 131 to 155 mph
5	More than 155 mph

Weather by the Numbers

The Saffir-Simpson Hurricane Wind Scale is used to rate hurricanes.

Hurricanes are rated.

They go from 1 to 5.

Ratings are based on wind speed.

Higher numbers are worse.

Katrina was a Category 3.

Floods were bad.

Millions lost homes.

1,833 people died.

Chapter 4
BLIZZARDS

Some people love snow.

Others think it is a pain.

It is cold.

Snow piles up.

Sometimes it can be dangerous too.

It was March 11, 1888.

The day was cold.

Snow fell.

Wind blew.

But this was not normal.

It was a *blizzard*.

A huge storm had hit the east coast.

Wild Weather

It was so cold in 1932 that parts of Niagara Falls froze.

AFTER THE GREAT STORM, MARCH 13, 1888

The wind was strong.
It blew 80 mph.
Power lines fell.
Telephone wires snapped.
Fires started.
Snow flew.
Some places got 20 inches.
Others got 60.

Warm, moist air rises above cold air.

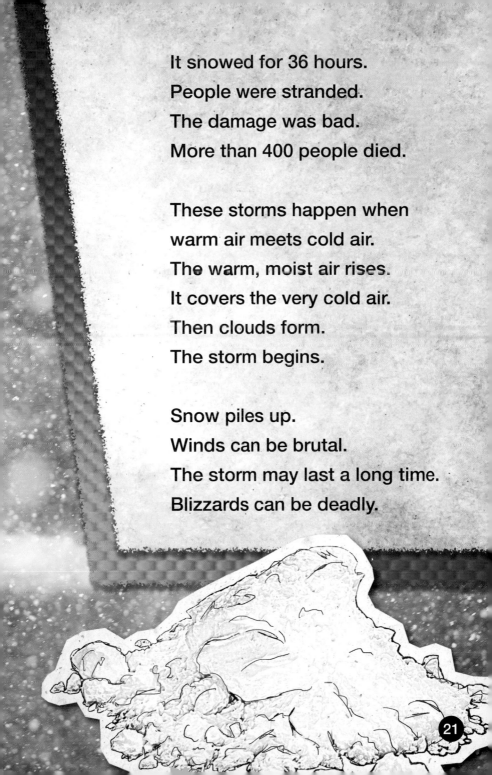

It snowed for 36 hours.
People were stranded.
The damage was bad.
More than 400 people died.

These storms happen when
warm air meets cold air.
The warm, moist air rises.
It covers the very cold air.
Then clouds form.
The storm begins.

Snow piles up.
Winds can be brutal.
The storm may last a long time.
Blizzards can be deadly.

Chapter 5
HAIL

Some storms have rain and ice.
Ice falls from the sky.
It is called *hail*.
Hail can be small.
Other times it is huge.

It was January 31, 2013.
Hail struck India.
This was not normal hail.
It was the size of boulders.

Hail fell from the sky.
People ran for cover.
It crushed crops.
Livestock was hit.
Homes were too.
Nine people died.

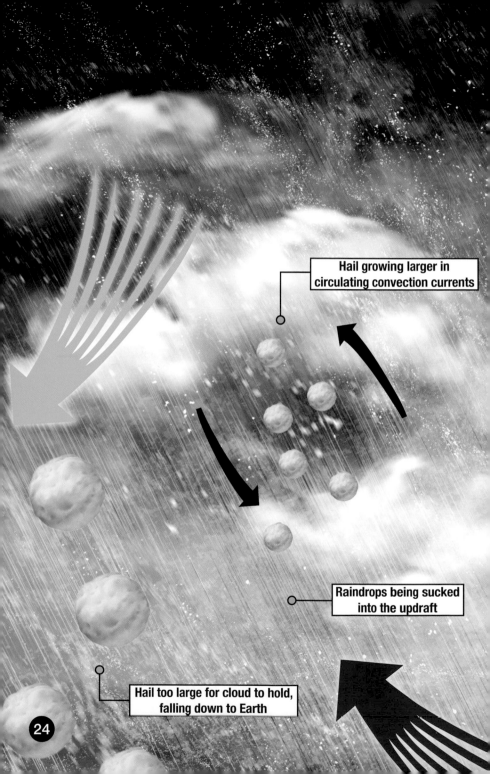

Hail growing larger in circulating convection currents

Raindrops being sucked into the updraft

Hail too large for cloud to hold, falling down to Earth

Hail falls from the sky.

It starts as a drop of water.

These droplets rise.

They go high in the sky.

The air is cold.

Water freezes.

It turns to ice.

The hail gets heavy.

It starts to fall.

Sometimes hail gets caught in a cycle.

It falls.

Then it gets trapped in an *updraft*.

More water goes with it.

It gets bigger.

The cycle repeats.

Finally it will get too heavy.

The draft cannot lift it anymore.

It will fall to the ground.

Watch out!

Weather by the Numbers

Some clouds can be six miles high. They can hold up to 500,000 tons of water.

Chapter 6
TSUNAMIS

Not all wet weather is from the sky.
Sometimes it comes from the ocean.

It was December 26, 2004.
There was an earthquake.
It was in the Indian Ocean.
The quake was bad.
It caused a *tsunami*.

Huge waves headed to land.
There was no warning system.
People did not know it was coming.
They could not get to safety.

The Indian Ocean on a map

A series of waves hit.
Some were 100 feet tall.
They slammed into the coast.
Water rushed inland.

Fourteen countries were hit.
More than 230,000 people died.
It was the deadliest in history.

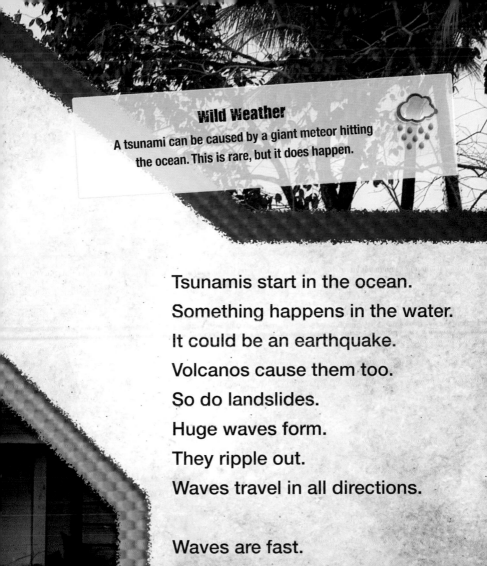

Wild Weather

A tsunami can be caused by a giant meteor hitting the ocean. This is rare, but it does happen.

Tsunamis start in the ocean.

Something happens in the water.

It could be an earthquake.

Volcanos cause them too.

So do landslides.

Huge waves form.

They ripple out.

Waves travel in all directions.

Waves are fast.

Some go 500 mph.

They slow as they move.

Some die out.

Others hit land.

Floods happen.

People die.

chapter 7
DROUGHTS

Not all wild weather is wet.
Sometimes there is no water.
Rain stops.
The ground dries out.
This is *drought*.

A drought is a period of dry weather.
It is not like other weather events.
Most happen at one time.
But droughts happen over time.

There is no rain.
Water runs low.
Crops dry up.
There is not much food.
People cannot eat.

The South Lake reservoir in California is at a low water level during drought.

East Africa suffers droughts.

The land is dry.

There is little rain.

Cattle die.

Crops cannot grow.

There is no food.

Millions suffer.

Many have had to leave.

Weather by the Numbers

Death Valley in California is one of the hottest places on Earth. The temperature once reached 134 degrees.

Some droughts are short.

They might be a few weeks.

Others are long.

They last for years.

chapter 8
DUST STORMS

Dry weather can have other problems.
Wind can make it dangerous.

It was September 23, 2009.
Red dust was everywhere.

This was in Sydney, Australia.
There was a *dust storm*.
It was the worst in 70 years.

Weather by the Numbers

Port Martin, Antarctica, is one of the windiest places in the world. The average wind speed is 40 miles per hour.

It started nearby.
The land was very dry.
A strong wind blew.
It picked up dust.
The wind carried it.
It went hundreds of miles.

Planes could not fly.
People could not breathe.
Some went to the hospital.
Others stayed inside.

Dust storms are strong.
Some last a few minutes.
Others blow for days.

How do these happen?
The ground is dry.
The soil is loose.
A strong wind blows.
Dust gets picked up.
It can travel far.

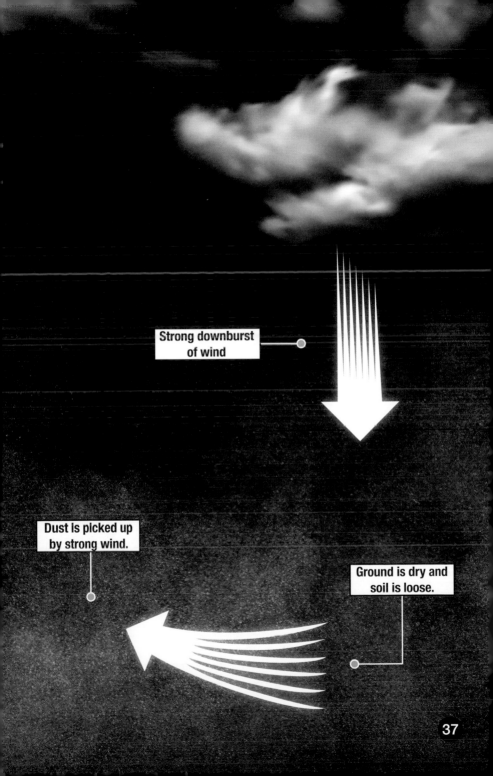

Strong downburst of wind

Dust is picked up by strong wind.

Ground is dry and soil is loose.

chapter 9
TORNADOS

Tornados are wind storms.
Sometimes there is rain.
Other times there is not.

It was May 22, 2011.
Skies in Joplin, Missouri, were dark.
But it was not yet sunset.
It was a storm.
A tornado was coming.

It hit near Kansas City.
Then it went east.
It moved faster.

WARNING

An alert went out.
Sirens screamed.
People took cover.
They had only 20 minutes.
It was not enough time.

The tornado hit.

Winds were 200 mph.

Trees fell.

Cars were tossed.

Homes were wrecked.

Schools were too.

A hospital was hit.

Walls fell.

Windows blew out.

This is rare.

Hospitals are sturdy.

They are built to last.

The damage was bad.

158 people died.

Many were hurt.

7,500 homes were gone.

HOPE
HIGH SCHOOL

Joplin is in Tornado Alley.

Most tornados start here.

Why?

It is because of the weather patterns.

Warm, wet air moves north.

Cool, dry air heads south.

They meet.

The air is unstable.

It starts to spin.

This happens in the sky.

Warm air gets sucked up.

It keeps spinning.

A funnel grows.

Then it touches down.

Tornados are fast.

They can travel 250 mph.

The worst are even faster.

Some are small.

Others are thick.

Some last for seconds.

Others last an hour.

Most last a few minutes.

Tornados are rated.

They are EF0 to EF5.

It is based on wind.

EF0 is the weakest.

EF5 is the worst.

Joplin was an EF5.

TORNADO RATINGS

EF0	65–85 mph
EF1	86–110 mph
EF2	111–135 mph
EF3	136–165 mph
EF4	166–200 mph
EF5	>200 mph

Weather by the Numbers
The Enhanced Fujita Scale is used to rate tornados.

chapter 10
SAFETY FIRST

Weather is a part of life.

It happens every day.

We get used to it.

But sometimes it gets bad.

Wild weather happens.

What can you do?

Be ready.

Know your climate.

Weather is not the same everywhere.

It depends on where you live.

Keep up with the news.

Watch the forecast.

Listen for warnings.

Many places use social media.

They tell about danger.

Have a plan.

Know what to do.

There may not be much time.

Stay calm.

But act quickly.

It could save your life.

GLOSSARY

barometer: a tool that is used to measure air pressure and predict changes in weather

blizzard: a severe snowstorm

climate: weather patterns that are typical in an area

current: flow of air or water in the same direction

cyclone: a large, powerful, and dangerous storm that builds over the ocean

drought: a long time of little to no rain

dust storm: a powerful wind that carries clouds of dirt and sand across an area

evaporate: to change from a liquid into a gas

forecast: to predict what kind of weather will happen in the future based on data

hail: pieces of ice that fall from the sky like rain

hurricane: a large, powerful, and dangerous storm that builds over the ocean

levee: a wall built near water to prevent floods

meteorologist: a person who studies the science of atmosphere and weather

satellite: a machine in space that moves around the Earth, moon, sun, or other planets

thermometer: a tool that is used to measure temperature

tornado: a violent and dangerous storm where powerful winds move around a central point

tsunami: a very large wave that is usually caused by an earthquake

typhoon: a large, powerful, and dangerous storm that builds over the ocean

updraft: an upward flow of air

weather: the temperature and outside conditions at a certain time and place

COMET CATCHER

Chapter 2
WHAT ARE COMETS?

THE SCIENCE OF COMETS
Scientists believe that our solar system was created 4.6 billion years ago.

Our *solar system* is old.
Scientists have an idea.
This is called a *theory*.

It was long ago.
There was a cloud.
It was huge.
The cloud spun around.
Rocks were inside.
Dust, gas, and ice were too.

Our sun was made.
Planets were next.
Then came comets.
They came from what was left.

4

5

Comets are special.
Many think so.
They hold clues.
We can learn things.
How did life begin?

Some have an idea.
Comets flew in space.
They carried *carbon*.

Carbon is in all living things.
It is needed for life.
People have it.
Animals do too.
Even plants have it.

**Famous
Comets**
Comet McNaught
It was discovered in 2006. This
is one of the brightest comets that
has been found. In some places,
people could see it without a
telescope during the day. Comet
McNaught takes 92,600 years
to orbit the sun.

Carbon molecule structure

6

7

**Famous
Comets**
Hale-Bopp
It was discovered in 1995.
Scientists spotted it just outside
Jupiter's orbit. The brightness
made it easy for people to see
without a telescope. Hale-Bopp
was visible for a record
18 months.

Comets flew by Earth.
Some crashed.
They broke open.
Carbon was left.
It *bonded* with water.
Life began.

But we need proof.
Comets might have it.
This is one reason to study them.

8

9

red rhino books®

NONFICTION

9781680210736

9781680210316

BIOWEAPONS

LESLIE DUTEYN

9781680210729

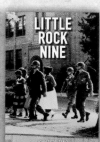

CANNIBAL ANIMALS

JOHN PERRITANO

9781680210484

CLONING

SUSAN HENNEBERG

9781680210347

COMET CATCHER

JOHN PERRITANO

9781680210477

DRONES
SUSAN HENNEBERG

9781680210293

FAULT LINES

JOHN PERRITANO

9781680210538

GNARLY
SPORTS INJURIES

JOHN PERRITANO

9781680210712

GREAT SPIES of the WORLD

JOHN PERRITANO

9781680210491

HACKED

M. G. HIGGINS

9781680210378

LITTLE ROCK NINE

JOHN PERRITANO

9781680210552

WWW.REDRHINOBOOKS.COM

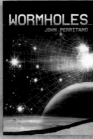